Martin Luther King Jr.

By Wil Mara

Consultants
Nanci R. Vargus, Ed.D.
Primary Multiage Teacher
Decatur Township Schools, Indianapolis, Indiana

Katharine A. Kane, Reading Specialist
Former Language Arts Coordinator
San Diego County Office of Education

Children's Press ®
A Division of Scholastic Inc.
New York Toronto London Auckland Sydney
Mexico City New Delhi Hong Kong
Danbury, Connecticut

Designer: Herman Adler Design
Photo Researcher: Caroline Anderson
The photo on the cover shows Martin Luther King Jr.

Library of Congress Cataloging-in-Publication Data

Mara, Wil.
  Martin Luther King, Jr. / by Wil Mara.
    p. cm. — (Rookie read-about biographies)
Includes index.
Summary: An easy-to-read biography about Martin Luther King, Jr. and how his efforts to stop racism affected society.
  ISBN 0-516-22517-0 (lib.bdg.)   0-516-27333-7 (pbk.)
  1. King, Martin Luther, Jr., 1929-1968—Juvenile literature. 2. African Americans—Biography—Juvenile literature. 3. Civil rights workers—United States—Biography—Juvenile literature. 4. Baptists—United States—Clergy—Biography—Juvenile literature. 5. African Americans—Civil rights—History—20th century—Juvenile literature. [1. King, Martin Luther, Jr., 1929-1968. 2. Civil rights workers. 3. Clergy. 4. African Americans—Biography.] I. Title. II. Series.
  E185.97.K5 M28 2002
  323'.092—dc21

                            2001006887

When we think of heroes,
we think of Dr. Martin
Luther King Jr.

4

Dr. Martin Luther King Jr. was an African-American man who worked hard to make life better for all Americans.

Dr. King was born in Atlanta, Georgia, in 1929. He was a very smart child. He finished high school earlier than his classmates.

Birth Home
Of
Martin L. King, Jr.

7

In college, Dr. King decided to become a minister. A minister is someone who teaches people about God.

All his life, Dr. King saw that many African Americans were treated badly just because they were black. This kind of treatment is called racism (RAY-sih-zuhm).

11

There was a lot of racism in the United States at the time. African Americans were not allowed to shop in the same stores as white people.

African-American children were not even allowed to go to the same schools as white children!

Dr. King spoke to large groups of people and told them racism was wrong. He led peaceful marches through the streets.

In 1963, he talked to more than 250,000 people in Washington, D.C. He said the words, "I have a dream." Dr. King's dream was to end racism. Those words became very famous.

Many people did not like
Dr. King. They sent him
letters saying they hated him.
Someone even threw a bomb
into his house.

19

Dr. King was brave. He never stopped trying to end racism. He asked the government (GUHV-urn-muhnt) to pass laws to help African Americans.

In 1964, the United States passed a new law. It was called the Civil Rights Act.

The Civil Rights Act said that African Americans had to be treated the same way as everyone else.

23

Dr. King spent the rest of his life trying to end racism. He was shot and killed in 1968 by someone who did not agree with him. Millions of people all over the world cried for him.

Today, we celebrate a holiday named for Dr. King. Martin Luther King Jr. Day is celebrated on the third Monday of January.

27

28

On this day, we remember Dr. King's dream to end racism. We also remember to try to make his dream come true.

Words You Know

government

hero

"I Have a Dream" speech

Martin Luther King Jr.

Martin Luther King Jr. Day

minister

peaceful marches

racism

31

Index

African Americans, 5, 10, 13, 21, 22
Atlanta, Georgia, 6
birth, 6
Civil Rights Act, 22
college, 9
death, 25
government, 21
"I Have a Dream" speech, 17
laws, 21–22
Martin Luther King Jr. Day, 26, 29
ministers, 9
peaceful marches, 14
racism, 10, 13, 14, 17, 25
schools, 6, 13
Washington, D.C., 17

About the Author

Wil Mara has written over fifty books. His works include both fiction and nonfiction for children and adults. He lives with his wife and three daughters in northern New Jersey.

Photo Credits

Photographs © 2002: AP/Wide World Photos : 28 (Win McNamee), 27, 31 top left (R.J. Oriez), cover, 12, 19; Archive Photos/Getty Images: 3, 30 top right; Corbis Images: 15, 31 bottom left (Bettmann), 7 (Bob Krist), 8, (Flip Schulke), 24; Hulton Archive/Getty Images: 11, 16, 30 bottom left, 31 bottom right; Magnum Photos: 4, 30 bottom right (Bob Adelman); National Archives: 20, 23, 30 top left.